I0488653

Killing it as
An Affiliate

A Beginner's Guide to Making

Big Money with Affiliate
Marketing

Table of Contents

Conclusion

© **Copyright 2015 by T. Whitmore. All rights reserved.**

This document is geared towards providing exact and reliable information in regards to the topic and issue covered. The publication is sold with the idea that the publisher is not required to render accounting, officially permitted, or otherwise, qualified services. If advice is necessary, legal or professional, a practiced individual in the profession should be ordered.

- From a Declaration of Principles which was accepted and approved equally by a Committee of the American Bar Association and a Committee of Publishers and Associations.

In no way is it legal to reproduce, duplicate, or transmit any part of this document in either electronic means or in printed format. Recording of this publication is strictly prohibited and any storage of this document is not allowed unless with written permission from the publisher. All rights reserved.

The information provided herein is stated to be truthful and consistent, in that any liability, in terms of inattention or otherwise, by any usage or abuse of any policies, processes, or directions contained within is the solitary and utter responsibility of the recipient reader. Under no circumstances will any legal responsibility or blame be held against the publisher for any reparation, damages, or monetary loss due to the information herein, either directly or indirectly.

Respective authors own all copyrights not held by the publisher.

The information herein is offered for informational purposes solely, and is universal as so. The presentation of the information is without contract or any type of guarantee assurance.

The trademarks that are used are without any consent, and the publication of the trademark is without permission or backing by the trademark owner. All trademarks and brands within this book are for clarifying purposes only and are the owned by the owners themselves, not affiliated with this document.

Introduction

Are you looking for ways to add more money to your income? Are you dreaming of one day quitting your job and focusing on your growing business? Do you want to create a stable passive income?

If your answer is "yes" to these questions, then this book might just be the answer to that!

In this day and age where commodities and the cost of living continue to rise, and an income from a single day job seems to not make ends meet, it would be wise if you look for other ways to earn money.

If you're looking for other means to add money to your bank, then you've purchased the right book. Before I go on, I'd like to thank and congratulate you for downloading, "Killing It as an Affiliate—A Beginner's Guide to Making Big Money with Affiliate Marketing".

I'm guessing that you downloaded this book, maybe because you've heard or read about affiliate marketing before and became curious about it, or you have a friend or a colleague who's into affiliate marketing and is already earning a modest income from it.

Like I said, if you want to know how you can earn from affiliate marketing, then this book can definitely help you with that.

I divided in this book into two parts. The first part will be like a crash course on affiliate marketing—what it is, its different types, how you can make money from it, misconceptions about it, and the reasons why you should be an affiliate marketer. The second part of this book will be more about the practical applications such as signing up for an affiliate program for your blog or website and YouTube channel like Google AdSense. There are also chapters in this book that will cover how you can grow your audience and drive traffic to your site. There's also a section here that will give you tips on how you can become a successful affiliate marketer.

Are you ready to start earning more with affiliate marketing? Move to the next page now! Enjoy reading!

Part 1: A Crash Course on Affiliate Marketing

The internet can arguably be considered as one of the greatest inventions of mankind. Since it was introduced, the internet has helped make communication much easier. Families and friends who live from different sides of the world can easily get in touch with each other through the internet. Accessing information is also made easier because of the internet. Gone are the days when people need to skim through hundreds of books and references just to gather the information they need. Because of the internet, we can simply type on a search engine, for example, Google.com, what we want to know and in seconds we are presented with thousands of articles and websites about the topic we're trying to search.

Of course, the internet didn't just make our personal lives easier, it also made a great impact in the world of commerce and business. A business from China who's selling consumer products, for example, can build their own website to promote their goods and also allow their customers from other parts of the world to order and purchase their merchandise.

The internet, through different online market sites also allowed not only companies, but also individuals to sell their goods online. The online market industry for example, allows individuals to earn thousands or even millions of dollars just by selling products through the internet.

If you come to think of it, the internet is not only good for communicating and research, but it is a great platform to earn money! Even in the late 90's people have already discovered ways on how they can make money from the internet, some have even able to establish a reputable business focused on just earning dollars online alone.

In fact, there are a 101 ways on how you can make money online. Some examples of this would be: getting paid to answer surveys, offering your services such as web development, graphics, or content writing, getting discount coupons just by searching the web, and earning money through affiliate marketing, which is one of the most popular means to earn money online.

What is Affiliate Marketing?

Affiliate marketing could simply be defined as a performance-based marketing where a company selling products or services pays an affiliate for every purchase a customer makes through the affiliate's advertisement or marketing efforts.

For example, you're an owner of a blogsite and you enlist your website with an affiliate program of a company. By being an affiliate of this company, you will be provided with ready-made links, or banners to place on your website. Depending on your agreement, the company will pay you for every sale closed, clicks, or leads that you can deliver the company through your link or advertisement banner.

Based on records, one of the first companies to set-up an affiliate program online is Amazon. In 1996, they launched what they call an "Associates Program" where affiliates could earn a percentage of the advertisement of Amazon they place on their website. Since then, this affiliate program of Amazon has been a model for many other businesses who wish to establish an affiliate program for their own.

Types of Affiliate Marketing

Pat Flynn, owner of the website www.smartpassivencome.com and one of the respected online marketing personalities today, identified three types of affiliate marketing, namely:

- **Unattached Affiliate Marketing**

  This type of affiliate marketing where you, the affiliate, do not have any participation or authority in the niche or product that you're promoting. The end consumer does not have any relationship with you, and all you're doing is providing a link, hoping that consumers will click on it and buy the product so you'll earn a percentage out of that sale. Flynn describes the affiliate of this type of program as "behind the scenes middle man".

- **Related Affiliate Marketing**

  Related affiliate marketing according to Flynn is when the affiliate owns a website, blog, or a podcast and then features products that are related to your industry or niche. For example, if your blog is on the medical niche, you may choose to place affiliate links that are medically related.

  But the promotion of these products doesn't necessarily mean that you actually use them. But instead, you just chose to be an affiliate of these products because your audience can relate to them.

- **Involved Affiliate Marketing**

Involved affiliate marketing is when you advertise or endorse a product that you use and you really believe in. And no, this type of affiliate marketing does not mean that you only place a banner ad or a link to your website. Involved affiliate marketing means you personally recommend the service or product to your audience in your content; either you write about it on your post or you mention it in your podcast or videos.

While according to Flynn, this is the most effective type of affiliate marketing to earn money, of course you also have to keep in mind that you have to build a reputable online presence first before people see you as an authority in recommending a product or service.

How Can I Earn with Affiliate Marketing?

Before we answer that question, I'd like to remind you that affiliate marketing is not a means for you to earn money in just a snap. Signing up for an affiliate program will not add money to your bank overnight, however, it takes hard work, dedication, and patience before you can actually earn a modest income from it. But yes, you definitely can earn money with affiliate marketing. In fact, Pat Flynn shares in his blog that he makes at least $5,000 a month just on affiliate commissions alone; this is besides the income he makes selling his products online.

Now let's go to the question, "How can I earn with affiliate marketing?" Well the answer here is simple.

First, you have to join an affiliate program (I will provide you with a list of these programs later), and then choose which products you want to sell. Once you've decided what products or services you want to market, the *seller* (a.k.a. the company/business) will provide you with a unique code that you can use to drive traffic to the seller's site. The sellers usually provide you, the *affiliate,* with links, ad banners, or codes that you could simply copy and paste to your website or blog.

An affiliate earns money when the users are redirected to the seller's site and then purchases a product or a service; this is what you call a *pay per sale.* It may sound like a long shot before you can earn money since customers should make a purchase first before you earn a commission, but the good thing is that there are some affiliate programs that pay you money even if you close a deal or not.

There's another payment term, called *pay per click that* earns you money just by redirecting a user from your website to the seller's website. There is also what you call *pay per lead* which refers to the payment term where you get paid once the visitors provide the seller their contact information by signing up on a contact form.

The sellers can track your performance through what they call as an "affiliate cookie" that credits the affiliate every time a sale is made through the affiliate links. Sellers usually keep a record of an affiliate's performance so they can easily track their sales and commission statistics. After every month (usually), sellers will pay the affiliates based on their sales or referrals.

Why Should I Be An Affiliate Marketer?

If you're still not sure about the idea of earning money from affiliate marketing, listed below are more reasons why you should start dabbling with affiliate marketing.

- **No need for large monetary investments**- first and foremost, affiliate marketing is a business, and this is one of the few businesses that don't require you to shell out a huge monetary investment. All you need is to do is to market a product or a service that already exists or is already developed by the merchant. You don't need to set up a physical office space or even hire employees to sell products. All you need is to direct your website's visitors to the seller's site to make money.

- **No needs to worry about logistics, storage, and customer support- since you're** only acting as an avenue or the middleman who markets the seller's products or services, you don't have to worry about all the dirty work that comes with the business such as storage, logistics, and dealing with customer complaints; the merchant does all that. All you have to focus on is how you encourage the readers to visit the seller's site and to purchase or sign-up for their products.

- **A good means for a passive income**- when you are able to set-up a steady flow of income through your affiliate links, money will just keep coming to you even if you're not constantly tweaking or monitoring your performance as an affiliate. There are some affiliate programs out there that requires minimal effort from you, but can still bring you a modest amount of income.

- **You can leave your day job and start working at home**- individuals who are really serious about affiliate marketing can focus on this business alone, leave their 9 to 5 jobs and start earning good money online.

    Don't believe me? Mark Ling, who owns the blog affilorama.com started being an affiliate marketer in 1999. At first, he was making $50 a week, but as he focused on his strategies on how he could earn more, Ling is now reportedly earning a whopping $1,000,000 every year on affiliate marketing alone!

Zac Johnson, who runs a business called MoneyReign, Inc. and owns the blog zacjohnson.com, started in 1995. His blog alone has 15,000 subscribers, which helps him earn $2,000,000 every year on just his affiliate income.

Misconceptions About Affiliate Marketing

Learning about how much money you can earn through affiliate marketing may cause you to jump right into it. However, I'd like you to remind you that earning that much money does not come easy. Thinking that affiliate marketing will give you access to easy money is a total misconception because it takes hard work and dedication for you to earn well.

Here are the other misconceptions about affiliate marketing:

- **Affiliate marketing is only for those who understand tech stuff.** This is totally false. Even if you have little knowledge on how a software program works and just know the basics on how you set up a personal blog, you can still be an affiliate marketer. In fact, there are a couple of user-friendly affiliate programs out there for beginners like you. (I will share with you a list of some affiliate programs in Part 2 of this book.)

- **Earning through affiliate marketing doesn't require any effort.** While your earnings through affiliate marketing can be considered as a passive income, it doesn't mean that you would just place links on your blog and then forget about it. If you want to earn and eventually grow your income through affiliate marketing, you must at least provide great content on your site. Even if you have affiliate links in place and don't do anything to your website for a long period of time, your earnings from your affiliate links might come to a stop.

- **You can only earn money if you pick best-selling products.** This isn't necessarily true. Even if you've chosen to market a product that seems to be a best-seller, if this product doesn't relate to your niche, or you don't know much about what you're selling, then earning commissions might not be possible for you.

- **There is no more room left for new affiliate marketers.** Yes, it's true that there are a lot of websites and blogs out there that are already hosting several affiliate links, but that doesn't mean that there's no room left for newbies like you.

  This is where the strategy of focusing on affiliate programs that carry products or services that are related to your particular niche becomes effective. Not only are you focusing on marketing products that you know, but you're also providing your audience extra value because you're allowing them to discover services or products that are related to the niche that they find in your website.

  You see, you could also be these high-rolling affiliate marketers, only if you put an effort to build authority online, grow your audience, and strategize to earn money through affiliate marketing.

- **You need money to earn from affiliate marketing.** Like I said earlier, yes, you will need to spend a little to set up your website like buying a domain, but it doesn't mean that it will cost you a lot. In fact, you can build a website even with just $20! Since you're just starting out, there's no need for you to hire and pay people to create a design for your site. There are some platforms out there (which I will also discuss in Part 2) that allow you to establish your own for free, even without paying technical people to do that for you. All you have to do is to research more on how you can build a website that people would want to visit.

Part 2: Making Money with Affiliate Marketing

Now that you have an idea what affiliate marketing is all about, the next step is to actually sign-up for a program. There are many affiliate programs out there that you can join, however, not all can make you money. That's why you have to be wise in choosing which merchants you want to affiliate with. But before that, of course, you have to study the different types of affiliate programs you think might work for you. To help you with that, I've listed five affiliate programs that are most recommended by online marketing experts.

Affiliate Programs You Want to Check Out

1. <u>MOBE</u> – This is by far the best affiliate program that is out there today. They promote high quality products and pay big commissions. You don't have to create any products or talk to any customers. All you have to do is recommend the information products to other people who are interested in affiliate marketing. This program is where I make the most money with affiliate marketing so I suggest you go to http://mylicenserights.com and get started!

2. **Google AdSense**- simply called as AdSense, this affiliate program provides website owners/bloggers the ads posted by Google. The good thing about AdSense is that even if you're just starting as a blogger, you don't need to have a high traffic volume to your site to be approved as an affiliate. All you need is 100 unique visitors a day on your site to be an AdSense affiliate. You also have the options to earn money not only through posting ads, but you can also make commissions through search, videos, feed, etc. The

only thing you have to make sure of is that every article on your website should be unique. Your application as an affiliate might be rejected if even a single article on your blog is detected as plagiarized.

3. **Amazon Associates**- this is another affiliate program which is most recommended for beginners since Amazon has the best user-friendly program which is ideal for those who don't have much technical experience. Since Amazon is host to millions of products, you have a wide variety of categories that you can advertise on your website. However, the only catch is that Amazon only pays you 4% commission at first, which means that you have to draw in a large number of sales before you receive a modest amount of earnings.

4. **Commission Junction**- also called as CJ Affiliate, this program is like a one-stop shop for affiliates since almost all major sellers (over 3,000) have listed their programs on CJ. While the CJ Affiliate Program can give you an in-depth report on the affiliate's performance, however, beginners might find it hard to comprehend this report and use it to their advantage. Also, being a CJ Affiliate means that you need to constantly monitor your performance to make sure that you're really putting money in the bank through this affiliate program.

5. **ClickBank**- this affiliate program is ideal for those who are selling digital products. To date, there are 12,000 sellers on ClickBank, which gives you as much as 6,000 products to market on your website. Also, this program offers a high percentage of commissions where you can make 50%-75% with every sale. The only issue with ClickBank is that you have to be very careful not to choose product scams which can also be found on ClickBank.

6. **LinkShare**- Like Amazon, LinkShare has been around for years. What's unique about LinkShare is that they

provide their affiliates with HTML codes that allow the ads to rotate. This simple feature helps website owners to administer and optimize their websites better. The only thing about LinkShare is that it is smaller compared to CJ Affiliate, which means you have fewer chances on landing on a program that will earn you money.

Tips to Becoming a Successful Affiliate Marketer

So you already have an idea about the top affiliate programs in the market. What do need to do next? Do you sign up for every product or service that you find interesting or profitable? Do you settle on just placing these links on your website and nothing else? How do you become a successful affiliate marketer?

Here are tips to become successful in affiliate marketing:

1. Choose a specific niche for your blog/channel

The first and very foremost important thing that you'd want to focus on is the content of your blog, website, or YouTube channel. Before you can even become a successful affiliate marketer, of course, you want to get traffic either to your article or video. The bigger the audience you get, the more chances of you having people click on your affiliate links.

Yes, there are already millions of people who run their blogs and have their own YouTube channels, but if you focus on a specialized area on a specific niche, then you will surely be above the already existing channels out there. (I will discuss more tips on how you can drive traffic to your website later).

2. Do not try to promote everything

You might be overwhelmed after seeing how many merchants out there are offering affiliate programs and how much you can earn from marketing their products or services. Of course, your first impulse is to sign up to as many sellers out there right?

Wrong! You might be overwhelmed if you do this. Instead of signing up for plenty of affiliate programs, what you should do is to pick a handful of several merchants that you think meet the needs of your market. Also, another tip would be not to be carried away immediately on high commission offers of these programs. What you want is to choose a seller that has already built a reputation and offers quality products; because these products are the ones that are usually trusted and bought by the market.

3. Never promote anything you wouldn't use

If you're still establishing your presence online, it would be helpful from the beginning, you are already building and protecting your integrity. This does not only mean that you provide quality and original content to your audience, but also, you should make sure that you wouldn't endorse any products or services to your audience that you wouldn't use or buy.

4. Promote products or services that are relevant to your niche

Again, since there are thousands of sellers out there that offer great deals when it comes to affiliate commissions, you might be tempted to sign up on every good program you see. However, this does not mean that you're going to be successful in driving visitors to these links. One of the best strategies that you can do to ensure that people visiting your website will be interested in clicking the affiliate link you promote, is when it is relevant to your post. For example, if your blog is about "how to become a professional photographer", one of the programs you might want to consider is signing up for is a vendor selling cameras or camera accessories. Not only is this link relevant to your content, but it will definitely appeal to the people reading your blog.

5. Avoid placing too much ads on your website

Your audience will avoid visiting your website or blog if there are too many banner ads, more so, if you have pop-up ads containing your affiliate links appearing once in a while. Even if you want your audience to click on the links, you still want to be as smart as possible when you're placing them on your website. Anything that's too much, or can make the readers feel like you're shoving too many advertisements down their throats will have them avoiding your site.

6. Use involved affiliate marketing as much as possible

Remember the three different types of affiliate marketing that I shared with you in Part 1? Pat Flynn, who earns thousands of dollars from affiliate marketing commissions says that involved affiliate marketing is the most effective way to have your audience click on the links on your post.

You can do this by discussing in your article how this product or service is good and why they should purchase it. Endorse the product because you use it and you believe in it.

This type of affiliate marketing, of course, will help you earn more when you already have created an established presence on line. That's why building your integrity from the start is every important.

7. Review the results of the affiliate program

If you want to continually earn from affiliate marketing, you should also track the performance of the program even after signing up for it. Maybe at one time, the program you signed up for is running well, however, since there is competition, another vendor selling the same product and service might be out performing the seller you signed up for because it offers better products to the market. Of course, It would be wise for you to transfer to this program not only to make sure you're earning, but because it also offers better products and services.

8. Sign-up for different vendors

Yes, you don't want to have too many products or services on your website, but you also don't want to be signing up for only one vendor. What you want is to offer your audience variety, and you can find a smart way on how you can spread the links from these different sellers around the pages in your website.

9. Always aim for a quality and unique content

Remember that even if you want to earn through affiliate marketing, your number one goal of setting up a website, YouTube channel, or blog is to create a content that is unique and is of value to the readers or subscribers. This is the only way you can drive traffic to your website and then eventually to the affiliate links listed on your site.

Also, even if there are articles out there that are for re-posting, you still don't want to do this because like I said earlier, Google might detect your site to contain articles that are plagiarized which can cause your application for Google AdSense to be rejected.

10. Always post something fresh

You can always set up a static website then hope that it will drive traffic to your affiliate links even if it doesn't contain new content. However, websites with fresh content do better when it comes to their ranking in search engines. Of course, what you want to aim for is to be at least on the first page of Google when a user searches for the niche of your website. That's why, besides worrying about keywords and SEO, you also want to put fresh articles to your site at least one every week.

Now that you are armed with strategies to become a successful affiliate marketer, the next step is to actually create a channel that will draw people to your links. The following topics that we will cover will be about how you can create a website/blog that gets hits and a YouTube channel that gets subscribers.

Affiliate Marketing with Websites and Blogs

One of the most common ways to earn with affiliate marketing is using your website or blog to contain these links and banners. If you don't own a blog yet, it's never too late to build one.

If you purpose other than building an online presence is to monetize through blogging, then you can choose from the two of the most commonly used platforms which are WordPress.com and Blogger. These two can enable you to set-up your own blog or website for free and are both ideal for beginners. You can choose to use any of the two, it's just a matter of preference whether which one works for you.

WordPress is one of the most commonly used hosting platforms because it provides its users loads of themes and plugins where you can easily modify it into a mobile site. One of the advantages of using WordPress is that you don't need to acquire a hosting service or even download applications to run and build a website, all you need to focus on is the quality of your content.

Blogger on the other hand, is deemed to be more user friendly. Like WordPress, you can also customize the layout and theme of your website. There's no need to pay for any fees or any upgrades if you want to have a custom domain name for Blogger. You can also have different blogs in one dashboard using the same Google account. But the biggest advantage of using Blogger as a platform is that it is a company owned by Google, which means that you can have all the advantages that the search engine giant offers.

Here is a table to give you an even deeper perspective of the difference between using WordPress and Blogger.

	WordPress	Blogger
Interface	The revamp of the	Blogger's user

	WordPress interface in 2015 made it more attractive and colorful than the previous one. This also made going around WordPress easier and customizing it even more user-friendly.	interface is also easy to use. At the left hand side of the dash board, you can easily manage the posts, comments on the websites, and even monitor the stats of your blog.
Domain Name	You can create your own domain name with WordPress for free or pay a minimal fee of $18 per year for a custom domain name. However, if your blog or website is already hosted by a third party, you can also pay $13 per year to map it to WordPress.	Like in WordPress, you can also create a free domain name for your website. However, if you want to customize it, you have to purchase a domain from a third part provider such as GoDaddy.com, EasyDNS, and 1and1.
Storage	Compared to Blogger, WordPress offers a bigger storage for free at 3GB. However, if you need a bigger storage for that, you have to pay for a Premium account ($99 per year) to get an additional 10	Storage on Blogger is quite small since you only get 1GB for any type of account.

	GB worth of storage.	
Themes and Customization	There are hundreds of free themes for WordPress online and you can also buy premium themes for as low as $10. At WordPress you can also easily add plugins and widgets to add more variety in your website. You may also want to purchase premium or business WordPress accounts at $99 and $299 per year respectively. At this cost, you are given lots of storage space and choices to customize your website.	Users can change layouts and the look of the blogs when they use Blogger. However, they are limited to only a couple of templates. And you are also limited to uploading customized themes and third party plug-ins.

Choosing which platform to use for your website depends on you. You can weigh the pros and cons of using WordPress or Blogger for your site. But you have to also keep in mind that when you sign up to these platforms, it means that you only own the content of your website, but you don't have access to servers, etc. If you're planning to eventually have a self-hosted website, then you may opt to use WordPress instead of Blogger since migrating your content from WordPress to your new website is 100% compatible.

Google AdSense and Your Website

Like what I mentioned earlier, Google AdSense, or simply called AdSense, is one of the best ways to earn money through affiliate marketing. By signing up, AdSense will post ads on your website that are relevant to your content, so there's no need to choose which types or categories of products you want to market on your site. Of course, you also have the control in which ads you want to block and where you want to place them. Also, you can monitor your performance to see if you need to do some tweaking to increase your profit.

Even before you decide to sign up for Google AdSense, you have to have your website or blog up and running for at least 6 months, so make sure you have already posted some articles on your site. A website that is still under construction might have your application rejected by the AdSense team. You also have to be at least 18 years old to be eligible for their program, and lastly your website must follow the policies of the AdSense program. Some of the violations of these policies are encouraging your visitors to click on the links, the website publisher/blogger clicking on their own links, and having articles containing any material protected by copyright laws.

Getting Started

Step 1: Create a Google AdSense Account

It will be easier if you already have an existing Google account, but if not, AdSense will direct you to a page for you to create one.

You can sign-up here.

Step 2: Wait for Approval

After successfully signing up for an account, you will have to wait for the AdSense team (it may take a couple of days) to review your site and approve your application.

Step 3: Create Your Ads

When your application is approved, you can start logging into your account to get the HTML code that you will place on your website, which can be located at the "AdSense Setup". You can also have the ads appearing in your site to be automatically relevant to your content by going to the "AdSense for Content" link.

AdSense gives its affiliates the freedom to customize the appearance of the ads, change the font and colors of texts etc. Once you're done configuring, AdSense will provide you with an HTML code that you can copy and paste to your site.

There are different ways on how you can add this HTML code depending on which platform you use; whether it's WordPress, Blogger, Dreamweaver, etc. And you can easily find the tutorials online on how to do it.

Step 4: Earn Money

You have to be patient when it comes to the first payment of your commission because your account will still have to go under a verification process before AdSense starts paying you money.

To verify the accuracy of your account, AdSense will snail mail you a PIN to the indicated payment address when your earnings have reached $10. You will then have to input this PIN to verify your address.

You will only get paid when your account has reached the payment threshold which is $100. AdSense will not release any payment that is lower than this. If you reach this threshold at the end of the month, for example, February, there will be a 21-day payment period before you will receive the payment. So expect to receive the payment the following month.

If, however, you don't reach this threshold by month end, you don't have to worry because the money you earned will be credited for the next month.

Step 5: Track Your Earnings

If you want to stay on top of your earnings and ensure that you are making money out of AdSense, then you have to track your earnings. You can simply see this at the "Payment Reports" tab.

How to Drive More Traffic to Your Website

Becoming a successful affiliate marketer can only happen if you are able to drive traffic to your website. If there aren't any visitors in your website or blog, of course, there wouldn't be any people who are going to click on your affiliate links.

It would be really daunting to think that there are already millions of websites and blogs to compete with. However, with proper strategy and techniques you can still gain modest number of visitors to your site. You can follow these tips below to gain more traffic to your blog:

1. **Pick a specific topic**

   Like I said, there are already millions of blogs on the internet that you will compete with when it comes to having visitors clicking to your site. So you have to think of ways on how your website can stand out. One of the ways to make people visit your website is to offer a specific topic under a niche.

   For example, if you want to build a travel blog, instead of writing general articles about travel tips, why don't you instead write about how one can use Couch Surfing when traveling around the world? Have your articles revolve on this theme so that people who are interested with Couch Surfing will visit your website.

2. **Be smart in using keywords**

   Of course, this is basic, but some people forget how to properly use keywords in their posts by peppering their articles with keywords hoping that it will add more SEO value to their post.

   When you place keywords in your articles, make sure that they are relevant to the topic, not because you want to drive more traffic to your website. Remember, quality of the content still comes first if you want to gain a steady stream of visitors.

3. Be active on social media

Do not limit yourself to just your website alone. A lot of bloggers get their readers through social media where you can use photos or videos that will spark the interest of users and then provide a link to your website. Others establish Facebook groups where you can begin discussions and answer queries which will then direct them to visiting your site to learn more.

4. Create an email list

You will have more chances to have a steady traffic to your site when you have email send outs, at least every month that contains the new articles on your blog. You can get emails by asking first time visitors to submit their email address to get the latest content from your site, or even offer them an exclusive access to a page in your website in exchange for their contact information.

5. Guest blog in popular websites

One way to build reputation and add more traffic to your website is to guest blog in another website that already has a big audience. For example, if your blog is about alternative medicine, you can submit a piece to health websites who are willing to post your article. Of course, in exchange for the article, you can ask the website to allow you to post a link of your blog in your content.

YouTube and Affiliate Marketing

Besides writing posts for your blog or website, you can also establish an online presence and earn with affiliate marketing through YouTube. Of course, YouTube is a totally different platform than your blog. Here, instead of using typed words for your content, your videos will be your main concern.

You must have a Google account before you can set-up a YouTube channel. Once you have one and are already signed in to YouTube, you can click on the icon with three lines on the upper left of the screen and click on "My Channel". In this dashboard, you can upload, manage your videos and even add channel art. YouTube's dashboard is user-friendly and very easy to use.

Before you can gain lots of subscribers to your YouTube channel, of course you have to create video content that's going to stand out. You can either create how-to videos, product reviews, tutorials, post podcasts interviews, or you could even simply post entertaining videos that you know will turn viral. The most important thing to keep in mind is that you have to provide quality and videos that are of value to the readers.

YouTube and AdSense

Like a blog or website, you can also use your YouTube Channel to monetize using the AdSense program. However, you should take note that you cannot create a duplicate account if you already have an existing AdSense account. What you can do if you already have one is to associate your YouTube channel to an approved account. You can learn more about creating an AdSense account for your YouTube channel here.

How to Have More Subscribers on YouTube

You can also use YouTube to also bring more people to your website. However, if you're just focusing on having a YouTube channel alone, just like the blogs, you will get a chance to earn more money through affiliate marketing if you have plenty of people subscribing to your YouTube channel. Here are some tips to help you do that:

1. **Plan for Your Video**

   Just like what you do for articles you post on your blog, you also have to plan for your videos. You have to create a script to make sure the content won't steer away from your topic. Also, ensure that your videos are in good quality, so you also have to prepare for the production side of it.

2. **Upload Fresh Videos Frequently**

   The reason why people would want to sign up for your channel is because they like your content. And you want to keep your audience interested in you by giving them fresh content frequently. You can start by doing it once a month, or depending on your video upload calendar. The bottom line is that you need to have fresh content. Because if you fail to update your channel with new videos, you might just lose the numbers of your subscribers.

3. **Create Titles that will Spark Curiosity**

   With thousands of videos being uploaded daily, you will want to stand out by creating video titles that will spark the curiosity of the viewers. You can add a little bit of information on the description area, but you still don't want to give away the main content of your video.

4. Make Your Channel Visually Appealing

Of course, to draw people to subscribe for you channel, you want to make your page look appealing. The good thing is that you can customize the look of your channel just by tweaking some custom options on YouTube. You must remember that the look of your YouTube channel must be relevant to your brand or the reputation you are trying to build.

5. Have a Call to Action in Your Video

Some viewers may just come across your video after scrolling through the internet, so they still don't have any idea who you are and what you do. In order to have them subscribe to your channel, one thing you can do is to create a call to action in your video. You can either encourage them to subscribe to your page, share your video, or visit your website by mentioning it in your video, or have annotations with links to the sites you want them to visit in every video you make.

There are a lot more ways on how you can gain more subscribers in YouTube and have them click on the ads you place on your channel. Just be creative in doing it making sure that quality of your content is still the number one priority.

Conclusion

Thanks a lot for downloading this book, "Killing it as an Affiliate: A Beginner's Guide to Making Big Money with Affiliate Marketing". Affiliate marketing is one the best ways to make money and add to your income online. Although being an affiliate marketer is fairly easy, to be successful and earn a modest amount from it, you have to work hard and apply strategies that will make people want to click on the affiliate links that you provide.

I hope that you will use the strategies and tips that you learned from this book to make money through affiliate marketing. Do not be afraid if there are already thousands of people doing it. Just focus on your niche, pick a topic that would interest people to visit your blog or YouTube channel. Make sure you provide quality content above else. Slowly grow your audience and build a reputation that would make people feel that they can trust you. And once you're successful in doing this, you can then directly promote the products or services that you're marketing in your content.

I would also like to suggest that you start with http://mylicenserights.com if you are sincerely trying to make high commissions with affiliate marketing. I have tried many programs and MOBE has consistently paid me the most money simply by recommending their products to others, it's a no-brainer.

Don't let any excuses get you from starting to become an affiliate marketer today! A lot of people have been successful in earning extra income through affiliate marketing. You can do it too! Good luck!

www.ingramcontent.com/pod-product-compliance
Lightning Source LLC
Chambersburg PA
CBHW071554170526
45166CB00004B/1663